TYMZUP:

TICK TOCK

SEAN M^CDONALD, SR.

FAAD

FOREVER AND A DAY PUBLISHING, LLC

Published by

Forever and a Day Publishing, LLC.

Triangle, Virginia 22172

Special book excerpts or customized printings can also be created to fit specific needs. For details, write to the office of the FAAD Sales Manager: faadpublishing@gmail.com

The FAAD logo is a trademark of Forever and a Day Publishing, LLC.

ISBN Paperback 979-8-218-38203-2

10 9 8 7 6 5 4 3 2 1

Printed in the United States of America

Acknowledgements

I thank my Creator, God, and my Lord and Savior, Jesus Christ. I want to thank everyone who knows me and who influenced me enough to pursue my dream of publishing a book. In particular, my wife Antoinette J. McDonald, daughter Seani Moneek, daughter Nia A'Joi (stillborn 5.23.2004), and son Sean Anthony II, you four give my life more purpose. My mother, Inez M. Katzbeck (McDonald), without you I wouldn't be possible. My brother Norman L. McDonald, Sr., "life ain't nothin; but a meatball." My brother Homer McClung, Jr., "we're makin' memories baby." My shy-brother #1 Odell X. Ghafoor, "South (High) Bronx" will always be home. And finally, my family, the McDonald/Chandler family tree is only as strong as its deepest root and healthy as its longest and strongest branch.

Dedication

I dedicate this work to all of the foot soldiers who hold it down in the name of truth and infinite knowledge and potential. I stand on the shoulders of many generations of people. I want to thank all of you who have come before me to prepare the way so that I may toil the soil even further and fertilize a nation whose minds are progressive and productive. Thank you for allowing me to share your portal.

Table of Contents

◆AFFIRMATIONS◆

A Pledge of Self Esteem

I am a hero to many
And a failure to some,
But what really matters
As that I am the one.
Who has to live with me
For the rest of my days.
Seeing a lot of bright amber
And some dark gray days.

I will travel roads
Made by struggle and strife,
Prepared to do what it takes
To have a prosperous life.
Thoughts of tomorrow
Ponder my heart and brain,
Realizing how determined I am
To ease the strain.

I have made some key choices

And wise decisions,

All were made

To continue on my mission.

The mission for justice

That started as a dream,

Was realized only

by the power of Self Esteem

Assimilate

I see a window of opportunity ahead of we,
But at what price of humility?
In this humidity, thick air of oppression,
volunteering to be degraded seems less than
A desirable thing.

In fact, it seems dumb as hell,
I can't tell whether or not there are
Any good points of that A word,
You heard of someone that has
made good of making an
ASS
out of I,
Mi of Late?

ASSIMILATION

Assume for a minute that our reality
is worth celebrating,
Synthesize that thought with what we see
and do everyday.
Since it's hard to leave home
without the mask I'm forced to wear.
In many cases myself is someone else.
My purpose is clear to educate
 and reach the masses of us
In the trenches of truth that thrive
to tell the thousands of them.
Letting our egos loose and becoming
 armored with community
Almost seems utopic even though
that is where I've come from.
The only thing worth living for is the idea
or reality of freedom.
Instead of being satisfied with the status quo I,

in effect, change

Often enough to dust myself off and not let the

stench of this shit

Necessitate my need for association or

ASSIMILATION.

Control

Control of one's own person,
Is rooted in his mind.
Since society thinks different,
It stops the tie that binds.
Respect of others space
Is the idea that should be sought.

It's in the Golden Rule,
This livelihood is taught.
When we think of others, first
And the joy it brings to thee
Is when others 'll think of others
And share that joy with me.

Control will soon be granted,
But not as a private or particular vessel.
But as a shared community spirit
To cherish and nestle.

Jazz Song

I walked through that like a jazz song,
Stepping on every note of those sharp bars,
Of those conscious elevating euphoric lyrics
That mean what they say and say what they mean...

They take no prisoners
As we pluck the strings of the bass guitar
Before
We take a pause for the cause and sho' ya right,
Big pimpin'
With a limp in it,
That funky Cadillac playa music.

Or put me on the floor for a fast steppin'
straight dance
And see if the rhythms of the movement change any.
The revolution will not be televised,
But it sure will be talked about and sang about

In the church
In the club
On the street,
In bed...
With what sometimes may seem to be the enemy.
Betta' make sure nobody's peepin' over your shoulder
Plottin' on your creativity.
All money ain't legal G!

Snappin' fingers doesn't mean your flow is sick
Depends on its upper or downer hypnotic.
Keep that beat flowin' into my eardrum
And let the vibration tell me a story.
Old as the first page of history.

Writing an entry with every thought manifested,
Changing time for everyone who checks it.
Clockers on the blocks or on the stoops waitin'
Patience is a virtue
'Cause not everyone knows that time it is
Generations upon generations
Of deaf, dumb and blind kids.

What's the place you dream of

Pictures of the Harlem Renaissance.

Makes us committed to the verse that thirsts

Can't run fast enough or drink too much.

The fountain of youth

If you knew

Anything about a generation that was

X'd out of the plan.

My Zone

Step with me through my zone of writing verse.
Close the door behind you and
let's see what comes first.
Let me grab my Case of Logic,
so I can digest a dose.

I surf through pages of names
and thoughts put to beats.
Each and every one of these words has inspired me.
To write lyrics of my own that freeze
moments of time in my zone.

The fragrant smell of White Diamond incense
Bought from the brotha' wit' the sack
full of baseball caps, we cop.
I lie on the couch and reach out
with the remote to press play.

Kelly Price is the first on the marquee today.

I listen deliberately trying not to get caught

By her soulful sentences.

Continuing to write my thoughts until I finish them.

Wondering whether I should write

the trials of love I hear,

Or put the wall of the room down on the paper.

The constant beat of harmonious rhythms

Hold me as tight as the couch

That keeps me buoyant.

The third track starts

Before I put the pen to the page again.

My toes wrestle as I rub my feet together

Kelly's in the background

Tryin' to resist this brother.

She needs a healin' for her soul...

...And I need to get ready for tomorrow.

Tymzup

Tymzup for folks thinking we can't be...
At least a community
Of shakers and movers, producers!
Instead of ninety-eight percent consumers.

Tym'z trying to make my point clear
As that H20 liquid
As sharp as that blade we keep
cutting our own wrist with...
Quit it!

Tymzup for folks sitting in class
Watching tyme pass
Thinking there are no questions to ask.
Taking up space and air,
Reluctant to be a presence here.
Voices echoing from bodies,
Posing as authorities

On subject matter that affects our story.

There's no tyme for "I'm sorries," struggle with we.

Help to repaint the tapestry!

Tymzup when all the money is gone

No more flossin' to do, platinum to adorn.

Put the pedal to the metal

About these scores we have to settle.

Sit down let's talk business

And plan to raise up out of this abyss,

The devil's evil happiness...

Rocks that got cooked up

Now need to be divided

Among these people that invested

Are you interested?

Entrust it!

You guessed it!

Self-sufficient!

Tymzup!

Tymzup...

Big man or little dude trying to be him.

We have seeds to raise

And not a second to waste!

Tymzup!

Are you down...to prove we can do this?

Tick-tock...tick-tock...tick-tock...Tymzup

What is Being High?

Is it spending
Most of the time...
Pretending you're not?
Naw...it's taking time out
From the continuing madness
Which surrounds you.

The feeling that you escaped
The very thing
That you're bound by
Right now...
Think about it
And think about what it is like
To think while you are sober.

The truth
Is what it is,
Or is that a state of denial too?

Am I high?

Well why

Do you think I am confused,

As if I have it twisted!

Do you remember

what it is like

to plan to get high?

Taking cautious measures

To remember

This part of your budget.

Oh yeah,

Part of the reason you work

So hard

Is to –

Get the munchies.

Or to calm the jitters

Or just plain

Ease the pain!

Don't stop now!

Or did you just admit to yourself

That

You can't stop now,

Even if you wanted to.

This is what it is

Being high!

Wake up!

Or stay asleep!

What is This?

What is this,

A rebirth of an age?

When cats like Langston,

Gave birth on a page.

I watch young kids

Compose lyrics on paper,

Reminiscent of Biz Markie sayin'

"We caught the vapors."

Love Jones might've done it,

And we know Lauryn has skills

Levert,

The Roots,

Guy..."Let's Chill."

Gil Scott Heron noted,

"The revolution will not be televised!"

In small groups, cliques,
Wherever we could wear the disguise.
On the corner with brew and tree,
Climbing outstretched branches of poetry.

I'm proud to watch the talent produce lines,
Of what so many people contest is a waste of time.
Our stories compare on every topic of discussion,
Generation X
Is an ignorant assumption.
We re-generate the DNA of history
That has been given to us through poetry.

Listen to the sounds of life through the written word,
Appreciate the power we strain to unload.
Smile at the sight of groups of us walk together
Searching the world over to become even better.

In meter and in rhyme, in song and in speech
We still manage to walk to a common beat
Of the heart that continues to ask,
"What is this?"

◆POLITICAL◆

American: Are You?

Featuring Tawana Day

The year is nineteen-hundred and ninety-six.

Black people! Better realize we're in a helluva fix.

Take a moment!

Or borrow that which is not yours.

Who was it...

Lincoln that started,

"Four score..."

I'm still waiting

For the Emancipation Proclamation.

The only real emancipation

Is eternal salvation.

You've must've already arrived,

I'll see you when I get there.

As a matter of fact, where'd you come from?

Or who brought you here?

Forty acres and a mule,

Promised after emancipation

But when our numbers grew thick,

They started immigration.

American: Are You?

One fifth of a man,

A NEGROES only so high.

The other four-fifths of me

You deemed to deny.

No rights were given

And thought to be inhumane.

We asked to be respected

And treated the same.

Civil Rights, huh, if you will:

I am a bill,

Yes I'm only a bill;

And I'm sittin' here on Capitol Hill.

Oh-oh say if you will,

But you dare I am still

Just a bill

They are only amendments

And can be concealed.

American: Are You?

There's a war outside

Tryin' to enslave our minds!

Is this another, sign of the times?

They call us minorities

Made up of assimilations.

Look up the word A.M.E.R.I.C.A.N.:

Are Minorities Ever Represented

In Creating A Nation?

Life, love, and the pursuit of happiness!

Just who did they mean when they said this?

Aren't you bilingual or did you forget

about Black-English?

The language is "THE POWER" is in the language.

No matter who we are,

We all need to be soldiers,

Only knowledge can prepare us

For the New World Order.

Dealing with the Cards
I've Been Dealt

Don't trick me with that flim-flam,

"Get a degree young man!"

I already know it doesn't mean a damn.

The thing I don't understand is,

How do I dismiss the lie I've been told?

Now I'm a dealer of a worse education than I was sold.

I figured this was the best way that I could give back.

Bein' told and believin' that...

"I would make a difference because I am Black."

I know that I possess a power that is infinite.

But how do I manifest it,

When I am trapped in a system

that tries to condemn it?

This is the system of the American

Educational System,

Illuminati,
& all other secret orders.
We have to re-educate ourselves
and rid ourselves of this torture.

Wearing the mask
and seeing with my third eye,
has become a part of my everyday being.
Through sheets of paper
And sticks of chalk, I turn the lights
on the Illuminati.

Teaching these foot soldiers
To hold their own
And realize the world around them.
And to never underestimate the power
they have within the color of their skin.
Now I have accepted a mission that is not easy.
But my life is a present
Given through generations before me.

Trick-knowledge has surrounded us
before the apple in the Garden.
Wisdom allows us to hear the tricksters
And beg their pardon.

Circumventing this mental, physical prison
With its glass ceilings.
Taking the cards into our own hands
and begin doing the dealing.
I'm just dealing with the cards I've been dealt.

◆RELATIONSHIPS◆

Between Us

Between us I could never see us being friends,
Just call you up for the purpose of hittin' skins.
Might feel the same because of the narrow
train of thoughts,
"Think a different way," says the brothers I bought
Stock from in terms of advice and life lessons,
More brains and trains from tricklets,
Featherbacks I was guessin'.
Between Us
Age ain't nothin' but a number
Like times I hit it and brought thunder.
Lightning storms is as deep as I thought,
Not consequences like pain and broken hearts.
The electricity between you and me
Didn't have to be made between static-y sheets.
Between Us
Counsel on what's real is as true as my color,
Browns when it's between sisters and brothers.

It took a while to see you as someone else, proud

That I know you are the same one now.

I see you in a different light now that

I'm out of the dark,

Your collective breath of a revolution to spark.

Between Us

I am glad I met you again,

Having never known you as a friend.

Brains, personality, a whole package of gifts,

Refer to you as a sister, if I didn't I'd be remiss.

Stride for stride in the struggle to the finish,

You for me for you is how we'll win this.

Between Us

My sister I'm your brother

Let nothing in the world put asunder.

We, together have strength in our way,

Kings and queens see the length of our mane.

Between us, let's keep it this way.

Black Family

What happened to the Black family?

Did we start staying up late

Watching those psychic fakes?

Cleo's on the other side

Watching those devils take lives.

What happened to the Black family?

Did crack start creeping into our windows

And through our doors?

And yours?... And yours?

Is it the norm?

What happened to the Black family?

Did we start leaving home

Without having to represent it?

Young kids are cussing...

Young guns are hustling!

What happened to the Black family?
Do you know of those big places
Where big faces
Get all the attention
We can't seem to keep?

What happened to the Black family?
Did we accidentally start staying at the store too long
Until we decided not to come home at all?
We see each other in the street,
But hesitate to speak!

What happened to the Black family?
Did you stay downstairs
While she went upstairs
'Cause y'all can't stand each other?
But neither of you knows what for!

What happened to the Black family?
Did we stop caring somewhere?
Stopped looking for our family,
Denying our relationships
Like it was someone else's fault?

What happened to the Black family?

May continue happening

If we don't recognize what's real.

Do everything with a sense of purpose

And get in where we fit in!

Brethren

You helped raise me from a buck
When I was new to all of this.
I can't help but to appreciate
The fact that you did it.
Everything that I am
Is a manifestation
Of your dreams and wishes.

You never knew
Your feeling good or hurt
was a responsibility and a privilege.
Cutting down trees and people
That may stand or have stood
In the way
Of my blazing trails.

Our mother,

By herself,

Burnin' our behinds

Because she loved bringing us

Out of hell.

Six years apart

Is a long time for trial and error;

Making a way for your brethren.

All that we share

Including curiosities,

Fears,

Wonders and doubts;

Are signs of lovin'.

We're an army,

You and me,

Keepin' time

To march to a common beat

Called family.

Your seeds,

My nephews and nieces

Have a story to tell...

"My daddy is the best daddy"
Not because of what he did
But because of who he is,
He knows about family,
And we're proud
To be his kids.

If you do "time",
I do "time";
To reflect and plan
our next strategy
for battling the beast.

Your freedom
has been granted already,
the Creator
Has set your mental release.

Since you've been locked up;
I've been holdin' it down.
No one can say it better than you
"...it ain't nuthin' but a meatball."

Brotha' man,

You are on my mind

Motivating me,

That's all.

Do ya' thang!

Write that book

And share our story,

You know it needs to be heard.

Raised on free lunches,

Wilin' out in 'The Jungle',

Our part of the 'Burgh.

Poo-Poo, Pretty Norm...

Whatever folks know you by;

Your legacy lives on.

Had brotha's callin' me,

lil' Norm,

until I had to tell 'em,

"My name is Sean."

Cats don't know what our cipher is like,

Or understand how we get down...

My Brethren.

Candlelit Dinner Table

Hey babe,

How's about you?

Let me cook for you.

I know the way to a woman's heart too.

Look at me,

You know I pay attention to details

And even though my tenderness

is different from yours

I can still make you melt.

I'm sayin',

All I want to do is afford you a nice date.

Away from the big, mean world,

Filled with cats that hate.

To treat you like the mahogany royalty that you are,

Let me caress you, and massage you

And treat you

Like a star should be treated.

I know...

You've heard it before and...

here's an honest chance...

for you to hear it once more.

I mean,

I'm not into you just to flatter you or spend dough.

I much rather spend time with you,

Quiet nights alone.

Listening to words you say,

I find myself repeating,

You, rubbing off on me

And our styles keep complimenting.

I notice that I like to be with you
And I'll be honest,
Sharing feelings like these
Is breaking a long promise.

I've had with myself,
to not catch feelings,
But you attracted me to you
With your sensuality.

Now if you're wit' it,
Let's chill and have some fun.
Sit down at my table...
Dinner is done.

Daddy

I dare only to dream
Of what is going to be,
A lifetime of sharing
With you, your mommy, and me.

Your lifeline is a journey
Of thoughts and ideas manifested
Into reality of two-hundred and seventy days...
Conception was a good idea,
But omniscient intervention
Granted your retention.

Through our works of timing
And perfect aligning
With the moon and the stars
Your mother's earth
Will fertilize your growth
Until birth.

My seed is you
Chosen to multiple into two
And four
And even more
And at twelve weeks
You looked so sweet.

Smiling for the camera
Which captured your first cameo.
Not yet looking for a tooth,
Just ten fingers and ten toes.

A complexion of mahogany
Mixed with the cherry hue
Of your mother's roots
Is the first image I have of you.

Sean Jr. or Seani Moneek
Is the name you will bear.
To carry on the legacy
of your mother and father.

I never thought

I would experience the thrust and flush

Of feelings shoot through my heart

To know I am responsible for shaping your start.

In a world that has so many ills,

Yet in still...

I am, to the brim

Still filled

With love for you

Most definitely,

'Cause I'm going to be a daddy.

Late at Night

I lay in bed...
And think about what it would be like
To give you me.
Putting our hearts next to each,
So close,
That we only feel one beat.

Late At Night
When you are not here,
I am alone
And lonely as though orphaned.

Needing your closeness,
The feeling of your skin
Keeping me warm and breathing slowly
Breathing slowly
As I inhale and exhale
The air of love made.

Late At Night
Time has kept us
And time will keep is
In one place...Or another
Late At Night

It is my earnest,
Honest to God plea
That time will keep us together.
Late At Night

I have known love with you
And because of you,
But I have also known love
Without you!
And it may be necessary
To return your heart
Back to you.
Late At Night

I dream of

What once was

An eclectic flight of

Two black doves.

But as of late,

My wings seem to be broken;

And I can't fly!

But I am still floatin' floatin'

Down, down

Toward the ground below

Wonderin'

How fast I will hit rock bottom!

Hearin' cats standin' around me

Clownin' like

A yo' that chick got 'em.'

Late At Night

My head is twisted,

Headache is bangin',

'Cause all I do

Is hear your tired ass complainin'

Fuck that, these are my late nights,

Give 'em back!

Midnight

Featuring Antoinette McDonald

Touching what tastes like sweet southern
apples after a fall harvest festival-
Carnival rides with erotic impulses
when I see your silhouette.
Loving what's in between that
caramel and pecan hue
Color blinded by the red negligee,
the thigh high love overrides.
You became me became you.

As I look into your eyes of the beholder
holding what's mine which yours.
You keep time, tick tock, as we hear the beats
of both our hearts stop-start.
Keep going! Don't stop the music from playing
the song of love, of lust.
Of good vibrations, of my sensuality.

Loving the thickness of your rod fishing for pleasure and its satisfaction guaranteed.

So stiff, ready for the ride that is hard...

Candy that sweetens the tooth decay - Suga Dadday!

Thesaurus this!

Loving on varnished ebony only four legs and a table top holds us up.

Back firmly pressed like creased pants of pleasure.

Rubbing my head as thoughts are raced to my scalp.

My only sheen is life-giving and receiving packages of plant food,

chain of seeds that fertilize into daffodils and roses of miniature

golf balls that putt into your greenery.

OR

You can taste that which is nutritious like the vitamins that does a body good-

Real good like a six A report card, making the grades aren't hard.

Putting in work-a-holic for that which is good to the BONE! BONE! BONE!

Bony frame of souls intertwined, tangled as bangles on my arm,
A sort of fashion show me where your love overflows.

Flooded like a small village.
You make me shake, an eight, a disastrous earthquake.
Your lava falls down this volcano, you make me erupt.
Nuts bust a groove of honey roasted cashews and macadamias.
Your strawberries and cream covers all plus what's in between, the sheets.
As we make passion fruit salad with every bump and grind of the coffee,
I think my time is expiring.

Bulbs of sweat...drip..drop.
Don't stop...You make my Body Rock...
I can't take anymore!
Here's two more from the back, I can't front-that turns me on...
Off the chain how you throw that thang.

Piping hot juicy as you wanna be, loving me
eternally.
Keeping me sliced night after night rider am I...
As I lay down upon your chest.
Broad and strong, secure me in your arms of
chocolate
Anchors that hold me near.
I Love the Love We Love!
Forever!
Am I dreaming this reality?
Bites of orgasms tangle with my hue and your rod.
Black is mahogany - Now that's good wood!
Thick trunk, branches of veins catching every breeze
of your slow winds blowing slow...
Grind as we
Wind
Down
To
Earth
Our
Bodies
Become
One!

The Feeling

Once upon a time,
Not so long ago.
I met you and felt
The feeling of love.
The person you are
Enables a special glow.

A special flight taken
By two black doves.
My friendship with you
Is one I have always longed for.

Somewhere, someplace,
Our hearts are together.
Rocky times and happy times
Our friendship has endured.

This friendship we have
Will last forever.
Will we be together?
Shh...
Don't speak.

Just keep me in your heart
Even when you sleep.
I do,
and always will
have an agape love for you.

The Love of Friendship

The Love of Friendship
Is quite unique.
To find a special someone
Is a feat.
We travel miles upon miles
Through life's maze,
Bumping and brushing
The sides of many a face.

Through all walks of life,
It's hard for the mind to conceive,
Do I have any? Do I have one?
Searching through all those I know -
Finding none.

The Love of Friendship
Although I am discouraged,
I know my life is not a facade.

Because no matter who's around
I'll always have God.
Friendship is a fruitful entity
Which is always growing.
My love for God is a friendship
And that is worth knowing.

To have a friend
Is to be a friend.
It's really that simple
And not hard to comprehend.
God is love, truth
And forever a friend.

He's there day, night,
- thick and thin.
He's right by your side
Ready to listen.
His love and support
Are never distant.

As a friend,

I'll give you this small tip.

He is the love surrounding

The Love of Friendship!

The Voice of Despair

It's like you throw salt in my eyes,

To tell me I'm who you despise.

No reason but to get me mad.

And to show me that you are bad.

Our love should not be sinister,

Let's plan to see a minister.

I wrote words through tears in my eyes,

Because I am who you despise.

Why do I walk through life blindly?

Asking what my fate is going to be.

I am praying, hoping for change.

This one love, can drive me insane.

It will crush me to see you go,

But what I see now is a load.

Give me a vow to be silent,

You will make me to be violent.

I won't leave you and don't leave me,

But an honest love is my plea.

"I do", is how I pledge my love,

A love for you my sweet black dove.

For odd reasons I cry inside,

Missing you being by my side,

Come back to me, in an honest, caring, loving way.

Start now, right now let it be today.

Let our love shine like the sun

And float like a feather,

Or be gone from me,

Far away,

Forever and ever.

Wax

Can I,

Metaphorically speaking,

Be a candle for you;

To light up every inch of your life

And provide heat for your sustenance?

Burning constantly,

I don't shrink or become burnt out;

Instead I evolve into new forms.

Changing shape, but never purpose;

Which is to comfort you by sight, touch and feel.

Covering every inch of your body, me, waxin' it,

Sends lots of tiny tingles surging

through your system.

Simply running down the sides,
Finding crevasses to explore and become molded
Into the very shapes that make you YOU,
and thus me ~Wax~

You see me as light that escorts you,
Through tight corridors and vast gullies.

However, if it weren't for your hand
that holds me high,
High as your head and stretched out
as far as your eyes can see,
There would be no me.

No purpose for burning or to be held.
Hence, my need for you is simple and constant,
You keep me focused on my purpose
and not my problems
But my privileges and my promises.

To be the beacon for you,
Can you see me? Can you use me?
Do you need me? Nothing more than mere ~Wax~

When my exterior is hard, I am not as malleable
As when I am soft, squeezable and mushy.
My dexterity is adaptable to the heat of the moment.

When I am cold I am still burning
with desire to be used,
To be touched, to be needed.
When I am turned on, ignited,
I'm softer to your touch,
I respond with a more humble, happy,
hurried to harden.

So I can melt ~And harden~
And melt ~Wax~

What is Love?

Love is an emotion
As vast as an ocean
That calms as it awakes
That few people escape.
"What is Love?"

Love is a duration
Without destination
You're not going to know
Just learning as you grow.
"What is Love?"

Love is of joys and fears
Seen through streaky blurred tears
The scene is chaotic
When you are deep in it.
"What is Love?"

Love is a special gift
That tries hard to uplift
The mind, body, and soul
Without a dreadful toll.